THE STORY OF

LAURA INGALLS WILDER,

Pioneer Girl

THE STORY OF

LAURA INGALLS WILDER, Pioneer Girl

BY MEGAN STINE
ILLUSTRATED BY MARCY DUNN RAMSEY

A YEARLING BOOK

ABOUT THIS BOOK

The events described in this book are true. They have been carefully researched and excerpted from authentic autobiographies, writings, and commentaries. No part of this biography has been fictionalized.

To learn more about Laura Ingalls Wilder, ask your librarian to recommend other fine books you might read.

Published by
Dell Publishing
a division of
Bantam Doubleday Dell Publishing Group, Inc.
1540 Broadway
New York, New York 10036

The trademark Yearling® is registered in the U.S. Patent and Trademark Office.
The trademark Dell® is registered in the U.S. Patent and Trademark Office.

ISBN: 0-440-40578-5

Published by arrangement with Parachute Press, Inc.
Printed in the United States of America
September 1992

10   9   8   7   6   5   4   3

Contents

For my father,
who gave me his love of language and an
enduring belief in the power of words.

Acknowledgments

Ever since the Little House books were first published, people have wanted to know more about Laura Ingalls Wilder. Some people have spent years researching her life. Others have become amateur detectives, trying to track down the routes that Laura took as she moved west. And a few have even gone to the prairie and tried to find the original Little House — or at least the place where it once stood.

All of that work has helped me in writing this biography. Two writers in particular are known for their thorough research about Laura, and I am grateful to them. They are Donald Zochert and William T. Anderson. Also, other than the Little House series, Laura wrote many books and articles about herself that I have used in my research. And Laura's daughter Rose wrote articles about her mother that helped me understand even more about Laura's life.

If you want to learn more about Laura, you

can visit or write to the Laura Ingalls Wilder Museum, at Rt. 1, Box 24, Mansfield, Missouri 65704. The museum is located in the house Laura and Almanzo built on Rocky Ridge Farm and is filled with many of Laura's own things. Pamphlets written by William T. Anderson about Laura, Almanzo, Rose, and the other family members are also available at the museum.

You may also visit or write to the Laura Ingalls Wilder Memorial Society, Inc., at Box 344, De Smet, South Dakota 57231. The De Smet society maintains museums in the original surveyor's house and in Ma and Pa Ingalls' house. The society also displays many of the Ingallses', Laura's, and Rose Wilder Lane's things and has an excellent bookstore.

And finally, you might want to read Donald Zochert's biography, *Laura: The Life of Laura Ingalls Wilder*, and William Anderson's *A Little House Sampler*.

Back to the Big Woods

"Laura!"

It was only one word, but it was enough. When Ma said her name so sharply, Laura knew immediately what it meant. Be quiet, be still, and stop being naughty. Now!

Laura sat back on the wooden seat and squeezed her hands tightly together in her lap. "Are we there yet?" she wanted to say. "Can we stop and camp soon? When are we ever, ever going to be there?"

But Laura didn't say any of these things out loud. She just complained silently to herself as the covered wagon rolled slowly across the prairie.

After crossing the wide and turbulent Mississippi River, the family traveled until they came to a thick woods. A little house appeared in the distance.

Whose house was it? Laura wondered. Did anyone live there? Could this be the little house in the Big Woods that Ma and Pa talked so much about?

Laura Ingalls was only four years old. She

didn't remember the first house she had lived in, the house in the Big Woods. Ma and Pa had left there when she was a year old. They had moved west and built the little house on the prairie in Indian Territory. Now they were coming back to the Big Woods after three exciting years.

The house on the prairie had been wonderful. It was a log house, and Pa built it himself with his own two hands. Laura loved living there, even though there were angry Indians, howling wolves, and other dangers all around them. Together with Ma and Pa and Mary and baby Carrie, Laura was happy in that snug little house.

But Ma and Pa had made a mistake when they settled in Indian Territory. The land rightfully belonged to the Indians. So Pa was forced to give up the house.

Now they were heading back home. Home to the Big Woods. Home to the very first of the little houses. And it seemed to be taking forever.

Laura fidgeted in the covered wagon. "When are we going to get there?" she wanted to ask.

Of course Laura's older sister Mary knew the answer. Mary was old enough to remember the Big Woods. And even if she didn't, she would never have fidgeted or asked questions all the time the way Laura often did.

Mary was six years old, and she was the opposite of Laura. She always followed the rules. Mary knew that children must not speak unless spoken to. She knew that nice little girls always walked and never ran. She knew that on Sundays children could not be playful or silly. They must be quiet, calm, and polite.

Mary was almost always quiet and polite. Unlike Laura, she never got her dress dirty or lost her hair ribbons.

Laura loved her older sister. But sometimes she hated the fact that Mary was so good. Especially now, when Laura was bursting to find out when they were ever going to get home.

It was May of 1871. For many days now the wagon had been rolling over flat, sandy ground under an enormous blue sky. But finally they went through the town of Pepin, Wisconsin. A beautiful lake stood at the edge of the town. Or really it was the other way around — the tiny town of Pepin stood at the edge of the huge, beautiful lake. A few miles away, deep in the Big Woods, a little house was waiting.

Laura didn't know it yet, but the little log cabin in the distance *was* home.

To Laura's surprise, something else was waiting in the Big Woods, too. Relatives! Grandma and Grandpa Ingalls were there, waiting to welcome Laura and her family. So were Laura's aunts and uncles and lots of cousins. Laura hadn't seen any of them for so long that she didn't really remember them.

Now, all of a sudden, they were hugging her and laughing and shouting and welcoming her home. Suddenly Laura had a big wonderful loving family. And they all lived nearby!

The little log house in the woods was wonderful, too. It was even better than the house on the prairie. There were three rooms instead of only one. Best of all, in the big main room there was something that always made Ma happy — real glass windows.

Outside the front door was a yard. Pa had cut down most of the trees to make a place where Laura and Mary could play. But two giant oak trees were left standing. Pa hung a swing from the limb of one oak. Laura could swing high in the air on the tree swing. And when she sat on the grass under the trees, she felt as though she were on a big green carpet. It was a perfect place to play.

Laura loved her house in the Big Woods. All her life she would remember this house as her first childhood home. She would remember having tea parties with Mary on the big green carpet under the trees. She would remember how safe and warm she felt at night, inside the little house with Pa and Ma. She would remember how Pa played the fiddle

and sang songs by the fire. And one day she would grow up to write stories about all the things she remembered.

But Laura didn't know that yet. Right now she was just a little girl, trying to be good. And it was always so hard for Laura to be good.

One time when she was still very little, Laura was especially naughty. As an adult Laura would write about what had happened in her book, *Little House in the Big Woods*. Her Aunt Lotty was coming for a visit. Laura wanted to look pretty for the party. So she stood still and let Ma comb her brown hair into curls. But even when her hair was curled, Laura thought that Mary's hair was prettier.

Mary's hair was golden. And it was *always* curled. Laura was very jealous of Mary's hair. She wanted Aunt Lotty to like her hair best.

When Aunt Lotty arrived, Laura and Mary ran into the front yard to greet her. "Which do you like best?" Mary asked. "Brown curls or golden curls?"

Kindly, and with a smile, Aunt Lotty said she liked both kinds of curls best. Laura felt so happy she wanted to dance and play. But when Aunt Lotty was gone, Laura and Mary quarreled. They were both tired and cranky. Mary said that Aunt Lotty really liked Mary's hair best.

"Golden curls are much prettier than brown!" Mary said.

6

In a flash, Laura's hand flew out at her sister's face. She slapped Mary hard.

This time Ma didn't say "Laura!" Pa didn't speak sharply either. He just said, "Come here, Laura."

In a calm voice, Pa repeated the rule that Laura knew well. The girls must never strike each other. It didn't matter what Mary had said to her. Laura must obey the rule.

Then Pa took a strap and whipped Laura with it. She sobbed and sobbed as if her heart would break.

The little house in the Big Woods was suddenly much too small. There was no place for Laura to go, no place to hide and cry. Laura sat on a chair in the corner and felt miserable.

After a while Pa said again, "Come here, Laura." Her heart melted when she heard the kindness in his voice. Pa pulled her onto his lap to comfort her. As his big strong arms surrounded her, she felt that everything was all right again. Pa had always understood Laura.

"You don't like golden hair better than brown, do you, Pa?" Laura asked.

Pa hugged her a little harder. "Well, Laura," he said with shining eyes, "my hair is brown."

That was true! Laura thought. Pa's hair was brown! And his beautiful long whiskers were brown. And Laura loved Pa, and she loved brown hair, and everything was wonderful.

She snuggled into his arms, putting her small head on his shoulder. With Pa around, nothing could ever be unhappy again.

Laura's Pa

There was always a lot of work to be done when the Ingalls family lived in the big woods.

Laura liked to watch Ma make butter and cheese from their cow's milk. She watched the bread-making and baking. Sometimes Laura even helped, making her own little cookies and pies.

She watched Ma make candles and hats, candy, clothes, mittens, quilts, brooms, and dolls. In fact, Ma made just about everything the family needed.

But even more than watching Ma, Laura liked watching Pa work. He was a skilled carpenter and built all of their furniture himself. He was an expert hunter and could almost always find game in the forest.

Pa's gun held only one bullet and it took several minutes to reload. So he had to be an expert marksman, able to kill a bear or a deer with a single shot. If he ever fired at a bear and missed, the bear would attack. Then Pa might be killed.

As far as Laura was concerned, Pa was good at

everything. When she looked up at him, with his shining blue eyes and his long woolly beard, her own eyes shined in return.

Best of all, Pa had a great joyous spirit and a love of adventure. At night, in front of the fireplace, he sang songs, told stories, and played the fiddle. Laura would eat popcorn and listen happily for hours.

Usually, when Pa was in a good mood, he sang happy songs like "Yankee Doodle" or told exciting stories about adventures in the Big Woods.

One story Laura particularly liked was about how Pa had been fooled and scared by the sound of a screech owl when he was a boy. Another story was about how Grandpa Ingalls had been chased by a panther in the woods.

But one night Pa took down his fiddle and played a song Laura had never heard before. The beginning went like this:

Shall auld acquaintance be forgot,
And never brought to mind?
Shall auld acquaintance be forgot,
And the days of auld lang syne?

When Laura asked what it meant, Pa told her that "auld lang syne" meant the days of long ago. But soon she realized that Pa's singing "auld lang syne" meant something else this time. It meant that

Pa and Ma were planning to leave the Big Woods. Pa knew he would miss the "old acquaintance" — their family and friends in the Big Woods. They would not be forgotten when Pa and Ma moved on.

Still, even though Pa would miss them, he wanted to go west. All his life, he had wanted to go west and find some land that was completely unsettled. He dreamed of being a homesteader — someone who lived on the land in an unexplored territory and earned the right to keep it.

Pa was a pioneer. And Laura was certainly her father's daughter. She was a pioneer girl! So the family made plans to leave.

When spring came, they would say good-bye to their family, to the little house in the Big Woods, and to the days of auld lang syne.

But before spring came there was a surprise.

Not all of Pa's relatives were going to stay behind. Uncle Peter had decided to go west, too. He was Pa's brother. And he was married to Ma's sister, Eliza. Their children were Laura's cousins — both ways.

So Ma packed up their dishes and clothes and a few small belongings. And Pa played a happier tune on his fiddle. Then the two families set out on the long trip west.

Traveling by covered wagon was a tricky business. If they left too soon, they would be battling the bitter cold. Every night they would have to sleep in the wagon with freezing winds and winter snows blowing all around them.

But if they left too late, the dangers were just as great. They had to cross the great Mississippi River while it was still frozen. If it had melted they would be stranded on the eastern bank for another whole year. Or worse yet, the ice might seem strong until the wagons were halfway across. Then it could crack and break under them. They would fall into the freezing river and drown.

Pa decided not to take any chances. They set out to cross the Mississippi in early February. The river was like a solid white highway running north and south. But Pa's wagon was headed in only one direction — west.

Laura wondered what they would do when they got to the other side. The air was still brutally cold. Would they have to sleep in the wagon for the rest of the winter? What would they eat? Most of all, would they be outside in the cold when her birthday came on February 7th?

To Laura's delight, Pa pulled the wagon into the town of Lake City, Minnesota. It was just across the river from the Big Woods. Now that they were across the river, there was no need to press on. They could rest for a few days and stay out of the cold.

Laura looked at the buildings in Lake City. She shivered with excitement more than she had with the freezing wind. There was a store in this town! She had been in a store in Pepin, and it was a wonderful place. Maybe they would visit the store in Lake City, too!

Then she could "look-at-but-not-touch" all the fancy goods that were for sale. Boots and shoes and bolts of bright calicoes in every color would be crowded in right next to brand new tools like axes, knives, and plows. Big wooden barrels would hold candy and nails. There would also be gunpowder, flour, tobacco, sugar, and tea.

But then Laura realized that something even more exciting was happening. Pa was driving the wagon toward a hotel! Laura had never stayed in a hotel before. This was where they were going to spend her birthday!

It was almost too good to be true. Laura nearly leaped out of her place under the blankets in the covered wagon. What an adventure this trip was turning out to be! No wonder Pa wanted to go west! Every day brought something new and exciting.

Ma, Pa, Laura, Mary, and baby Carrie stayed in the hotel for several days. Pa could afford this luxury because he had just sold his house in the Big Woods. He had almost a thousand dollars!

Of course he knew that he would need most of that money to get started when they reached their new homestead in the west. But even when he was poor, Pa always believed in having small treats for special occasions.

On this special occasion, Laura's seventh birthday, Pa bought her a little book of poetry. It was called a "Flowret."

Laura hugged the book closely to her, almost as if it were a doll. Now that she was seven, books were just as precious as any toy or doll could be. She had visited school with Mary, in the Big Woods. She could already read some of the words in her book.

And Laura knew she would be going to school again, once they were settled in the West. Pa had promised that to Ma. No matter where they homesteaded, it wouldn't be in a place so unsettled and uncivilized that it didn't have a school.

So Laura knew this book was just the beginning. It was only one glimpse into the many worlds she could visit through the magic of books.

A few days after her birthday, Pa pulled the wagons onto the trail again. It was still too cold to go far. They traveled a little way till they came to a little house at the edge of a creek. It was an empty, abandoned cabin. Anyone passing by could stop and sleep in it.

Pa and Uncle Peter immediately moved their two families into the empty log house. They made a fire in the fireplace. This would be a safe, warm, cheap place to stay until winter was truly over.

Laura fell asleep that night listening to a creek right outside her window. It was a soothing sound — the sound of water constantly moving on.

For Laura, the creek was like the life that lay ahead of her — sometimes clear, sometimes troubled and choppy, with an occasional rock or two. But always, always moving on.

Nine Moving Days

Laura didn't know that her moving days had just begun.

As soon as the weather was warm, Pa and Uncle Peter hitched their horses to the wagons again. For a while, the two Ingalls families traveled west across Minnesota. But Uncle Peter only went a short way.

Then he stopped and rented a farm. Pa was looking for more adventure, though. He was always looking westward — always itching to move on.

Where was Pa headed? No one could say for sure, not even Pa. All he wanted in the world was the chance to make his home where the country was wide open and free. Someplace where there weren't too many people. Someplace unsettled, where the opportunities seemed limitless, and a man could carve out a whole new life for himself by living off the land.

That was the life Pa was looking for.

And he thought he had found it when he had a chance to buy a small dugout house on the banks of Plum Creek.

Laura was not so sure that living in a dugout was going to be paradise, though. After all, a dugout was just a hole in the side of a hill. There was one tiny window covered with greased paper, not glass. Very little sunlight came in. And the dirt ceiling was covered with boughs and hay!

About the only thing Laura liked about the dugout was that she could go outside, climb up the knoll, and stand on the roof!

Summer passed quickly on Plum Creek. Laura spent every minute outside. She swam in the creek in her clothes, letting the water balloon her skirts up like a parachute to make her float. She rolled in the haystacks, even when Pa told her not to. She found plums on the ground along Plum Creek, and soon learned how to shake a plum tree just right, so that the ripe plums would fall off without loosening the green ones. She let the mud from the banks of the creek squish between her bare toes.

If there had been a school in the town nearby, Laura and Mary would have gone. Ma wanted them to learn so that, as she said, "they wouldn't grow up wild." But Walnut Grove, Minnesota, was so newly settled that a school hadn't been built yet. So Laura and Mary were free.

Laura didn't know it at the time, but these were some of the last completely carefree days of childhood she would ever know. The following year things began to change.

In the spring, Pa built a wonderful house on the prairie made with board lumber instead of logs. It had a door with real metal hinges instead of the leather straps he had used before. There were double hung glass windows that could be raised and lowered. And for Ma there was a brand new cookstove with four burners instead of one.

The only problem was that Pa had borrowed the money to pay for the house. He was going to pay it back when he sold his wheat crop at the end of the summer.

But one day the sky grew dark, as if a storm were coming. Laura, Mary, Ma, and Pa ran outside. They looked up and saw a strange-looking cloud — a terrible cloud of grasshoppers. Then one by one the grasshoppers started falling to the ground. They dropped on Laura and tumbled onto the house. They rained down like hailstones.

Soon every inch of ground was covered with grasshoppers. Laura's face and dress were alive with them. Everywhere she walked, she stepped on grasshoppers.

And then they began to eat Pa's wheat.

Within a day the entire crop was destroyed.

With it Pa's chances of paying for the house were destroyed, too.

To earn money, Pa had to do the one thing he hated most. He had to go east. To him, it was like going backward from his dreams. He walked for miles and miles in boots that had big holes in the soles. Ma, Laura, Mary, and Carrie were left all alone.

With Pa gone, there were so many chores to do that Laura and Mary had little time for playing. And they were all hungry, even the cow. Every single green blade of grass had been destroyed by the grasshoppers. There was nothing for the cattle to graze on. The cow got so thin her bones showed. She gave less milk, and what she did give was bitter.

The greatest hardship, though, was missing Pa. He was gone so long that the family wondered whether he would ever come back. Ma worried most, knowing that soon she was going to need him more than ever. Soon she was going to have another baby.

Finally they got a letter from Pa. He was safe! Ma breathed a sigh of relief. A few months later he came back. But when he returned, he decided it was time to move again.

This time he put the family into a little house in the town of Walnut Grove. Winter was coming, and Pa wanted them to be safe from the wild storms of the prairie. Also, the school had been built by now. Pa wanted to keep his promise to Ma. So Laura and Mary went to school.

In November, Ma's baby was born and named after Pa — Charles Frederick Ingalls. Laura and Mary called him Freddie.

For a while, it seemed as if life would be all right again. Maybe next spring there wouldn't be any grasshoppers. Maybe then the fields of wheat would overflow with golden grain and Pa would have bushels and bushels to sell. They would be rich!

The following spring they moved back into the wonderful new house with the many-paned glass windows. But then the grasshopper eggs began to hatch. Laura didn't have to ask what would happen now. She knew. The crops would be ruined, just as they had been last year. And all Pa's dreams of a pioneer life would be ruined, too.

Laura had moved four times in the last eighteen months. During the next year she would move five more times.

First, Pa sold the beautiful house in grasshopper country and they went back east to live with Uncle Peter. But Laura knew this was only temporary. Pa needed work, and Ma needed some help with the new baby. He was sick, and it seemed as though he would never get well.

Pa and Ma hoped that this stop along life's journey would bring them what they needed: a little money, a little comfort, and the energy to go on and try again. But instead they found only sadness. Baby Freddie's illness worsened. Finally, when he was nine months old, he died.

Pa and Ma were sick with grief. And another move lay ahead of them. As they pulled the wagon out of Peter Ingalls's yard, they were not only leaving behind their brother and sister. They were leaving behind their little baby, too. Laura had never known such misery as the day the family buried little Freddie.

What was more, they weren't even heading west, but south. Pa had met a man named Steadman. He owned a hotel in Burr Oak, Iowa, and Pa had promised to help him run it. So that's where they went next.

Somehow, the gloom seemed to follow them to Burr Oak, too. At first they lived in the hotel. Laura and Mary went to school during the day. After school, they helped out in the hotel, waiting on tables in the dining room. Sometimes Laura washed dishes.

But Ma didn't like the hotel because it had a

23

saloon. Men drank and gambled there. Someone had even shot a bullet hole through the dining room door! Ma didn't want Laura, Mary, or Carrie to see the behavior of the rowdy saloon customers.

So, for the sake of the girls, Pa rented some rooms above a grocery store. They lived there for only a few months before finding yet another home. It was a small house at the edge of the village, near the church.

Laura liked this house because it was close to town and yet not in it. In one direction, she could walk to school. In the other direction, she could walk to a little pasture that bordered a creek. Laura spent more time on the pasture side of the house, especially when the troubles at home felt like a weight on her soul.

One day a wealthy woman came to visit Ma. She explained that her daughters had grown up and now she felt very lonely. It would be so nice, the woman said, to have a pleasant young girl living with her. The girl could help with the chores and keep her company. She made it clear that she was rich enough to provide a good life for such a lucky little girl.

Laura stood and listened in horror. This woman didn't want just any girl to come live with her. She wanted *Laura* — wanted her as an adopted daughter! Laura's heart almost stopped when the woman asked Ma outright if she would give Laura up.

It seemed like an eternity before Ma gave her answer. Perhaps Ma was not sure what she should do. Would Laura be happier, or better off, living with a wealthy family? Would it be easier for Ma and Pa with one less mouth to feed? Poor families often did give up a child, especially when money was short and times were hard.

But one look at Laura's face was all it took for Ma to decide. No, she told the woman, she couldn't possibly let Laura go. She was needed too much at home. Laura knew that Ma also meant she was loved too much, too.

It was not a happy year for Laura. But there were a few bright moments. One day in May, Ma and Pa sent her on an errand that took a particularly long time. When she returned, she found that another baby had been born in the Ingalls household. Ma and Pa named her Grace.

It had always been like that when Ma's babies were born. Somehow Pa would find a way to get Laura and Mary out of the house, without telling them why. When they came home, there was the baby — a wonderful surprise!

In the fall, when the baby was old enough to

travel, Pa decided to move again. They would leave Burr Oak and return to Plum Creek. Perhaps the grasshopper plague would be over. Perhaps not. By now, no one expected life to be easy, least of all Laura.

Almost Home

In one way, going back to Plum Creek was like going home. But in another way, no *place* felt like home to Laura.

Home was being with Ma and Pa, and listening to Pa playing songs on the fiddle. Home was walking through the prairie grass hand in hand with Mary. Home was telling stories around the fire at night, or going to church on Christmas Eve. Even when they were constantly traveling from place to place in the covered wagon, Laura felt that she was "home" because Ma, Pa, Mary, Carrie, and Grace were there.

Home was family and family was home, and that was all that mattered.

Still, it gave Laura a warm feeling to arrive back in Walnut Grove again after moving nine times in less than two years. The houses and the buildings were familiar, and when Laura started school that fall, her schoolmates were familiar, too.

But nothing ever stayed exactly the same.

That's what Laura was beginning to realize. For one thing, even though they had come back to Walnut Grove, they did not live in the wonderful house by Plum Creek. That house was already sold. So, until Pa could find work and build another house, Laura and her family lived with some old friends.

For another thing, now that Laura and Mary were growing up, Ma expected them to act like young ladies, not little girls. Laura was ten years old, almost eleven. Mary was twelve, going on thirteen.

Mary didn't mind acting like a young lady. She had always enjoyed being polite and showing off her good manners.

But Laura was just the opposite. She loved to be free. Sometimes that meant *wild* and free. In winter, Laura wanted to make hard-packed snowballs and have snowball fights with the boys in the school yard. When Ma told her that she must not have snowball fights at recess, Laura obeyed. After that, she only had snowball fights when she was walking home from school.

With pride and defiance, Laura Ingalls told her friends, "I can throw those snowballs just as fast and as hard as any boy!"

No wonder she was respected by all the girls at school. They admired her courage and independence, and they thought of her as the leader.

Whenever Laura stayed inside at recess, most of the other girls did, too.

When spring came, Pa built another house for the family. It was the fourth one he had built in thirteen years. It was in the corner of a pasture owned by a man named Masters. Mr. Masters owned the hotel in town, too. Pa liked him very much.

One summer when Laura was eleven, she was hired to work in Mr. Masters's hotel. Now that she was growing up, adults had begun to trust her with adult responsibilities. She washed dishes and waited on tables, just as she had in Burr Oak, Iowa. But this time Laura got paid. She earned 50 cents a week.

Even back then, that wasn't very much money. Pa could earn a dollar a day doing carpentry or farm labor. Just the same, Laura felt good about earning money. She gave it to Ma and Pa to help out with the family expenses.

By now Laura was earning a reputation as a responsible, trustworthy girl. So when someone in town needed extra help, they often thought of her.

One winter she was asked to come live with a family named Hurley. Sadie Hurley was sick, and her husband was too busy with his own work to take care of her. So they hired eleven-year-old Laura to cook and clean and wait on Sadie Hurley day and night.

The job lasted two long weeks, and Laura was desperately homesick. There was no one to talk to at the Hurleys' house, and no one to throw snowballs with. And even when she wasn't doing something for the Hurleys, Laura had her own schoolwork to do. She had to keep up with her schoolwork so that she wouldn't fall behind.

At night she slept in a corner of the front room behind a curtain. Lying there in the dark alone, Laura was so homesick she almost cried. When the two weeks were up, she practically ran back to Ma and Pa. It was so good to be home!

Then, one day, something terrible happened. It signaled once and for all that things could never stay the same.

Fourteen-year-old Mary got sick.

Sickness was nothing new to Laura. She and Mary and Ma and Pa had all been sick many times before. They had all had something they called "fever 'n' ague" — she later learned it was really malaria, a disease carried by mosquitoes. Another time, all the Ingalls children, including the cousins, had scarlet fever. Most recently, Laura and Mary had been sick with the measles. But that was several years ago. They had both gotten over it. Hadn't they?

Never mind about the past, Laura thought.

This was now. And now was terrible, frightening, and unexplainable.

Suddenly Mary had a terrible pain in her head. It was so severe that Ma and Pa stood watch over her. Their faces were lined with worry and grief.

Laura had seen that look on Ma's face before — when baby Freddie died. Mary wasn't going to die, was she? She just *couldn't* die.

But at the bottom of her heart Laura knew that Mary might. Pa and Ma thought so, too. Her fever was so high that she was delirious. She had strange, terrible dreams. She talked in her sleep — even when she seemed to be awake.

The town doctor came to see Mary regularly, but there wasn't much he could do. The fever just wouldn't come down.

For many years Laura had been jealous of Mary's beautiful golden curls. Now Laura watched in horror as Ma cut off all of Mary's hair. Ma thought it might make Mary's head cooler. Somehow she had to bring the fever down.

Finally, after many days, the fever broke. But everyone could see that Mary was not better yet. One side of her face was drawn out of shape, and when the doctor came, he told them why.

Mary had a stroke. And now she was going blind.

Silver Lake

Mary's blindness was like the end of a chapter in Laura's life. She and Mary would never again share experiences in the same way. They would never again be able to exchange their feelings with only a glance. They would never again exclaim at the same moment about the shimmering colors on a lake at sunset. And they would never again go off hand in hand to school. For now that she was blind, Mary could not go to school.

Of course Laura loved Mary as much as ever. And she admired her sister more now, too. All through her illness, Mary had never complained, no matter how awful she felt. And when the blindness came, she was terribly brave — even though she had never been brave about trouble before.

Maybe Mary wasn't so different from her after all, Laura thought. Laura decided that from now on she would try even harder to be like Mary — to be good.

And from now on, Pa said, Laura would have

to be Mary's eyes. She would have to do her seeing for her, describing the world for Mary, painting pictures with words.

One day Laura saw a strange woman standing at the door. Laura described her for Mary, mentioning her brown print dress and sunbonnet. Laura didn't know who the woman was, and Mary couldn't recognize her from the description. But Ma knew. It was Laura's Aunt Docia, who had traveled all the way to Minnesota from the Big Woods.

Aunt Docia had come for a special reason. She was on her way to meet her new husband in the Dakotas, and she wanted Pa to come, too. She offered Pa a job. He could work for her husband in the western camps where the railroad was being built.

Pa's whole face lit up when he heard the offer, and his blue eyes twinkled. A chance to go west again? And be a homesteader? It sounded great! This was exactly what Pa needed, what he had been dreaming of for years. Maybe this time they would find happiness and peace of mind.

But Ma did not want to pick up and move again. What she wanted was a permanent home in a civilized town. She wanted good schools for her daughters and a good church for the family. In the West, there would be no schools and no church. In fact there would be no town. Aunt Docia was talking about a place so far west that it wasn't even settled yet.

Laura's opinion didn't matter to Ma and Pa, so she didn't give it. But inside, she was desperately hoping that Ma would agree to the move. After all, Laura was a pioneer girl. She wanted what Pa wanted — to wander free, and explore the vast wilderness of untamed America.

Finally, Ma and Pa made a bargain. Ma agreed to go west to Dakota. Pa promised that this would be the last time he ever asked her to move. Ever.

It was a long time before the family was finally settled in the new territory. First Pa went alone in the covered wagon — he was needed at the railroad camps right away. A few months later Ma, Mary, Laura, Carrie, and Grace joined him, traveling by train.

From the first day of the trip, Laura kept busy describing things for Mary. She named the color of the red velvet seats in the train, although Mary could feel the texture herself. She described the train conductor's uniform, although Mary could tell that the man was tall because his voice was so "high up."

Then Laura tried to tell Mary about the scenery whizzing past the big plate glass windows. But it was moving so quickly that Laura couldn't take it all in.

The land here was not like the prairies Laura had seen all her life. There was the endless blue sky and the endless waving prairie grass — that was the same. But there seemed to be so much, much more of it. With few creeks or streams and without a tree in sight, the prairie looked as though it went on forever. Laura felt very small and alone.

She was learning that being a pioneer meant going into a totally unsettled territory, beyond the end of the railroad line. It meant living where there was no sheriff to keep law and order and no neighbors to become friends with.

All the railroad workers would move on when the tracks were laid. The Ingalls would be the very first people to build a house and settle down in this part of the world.

They were starting a town.

That's how it always was in the 1870s when the railroad was being built. After each section was finished, men would map out a few streets for a town and the workers would push on. The railroad was always pushing west, the men were always laying more track, and the towns grew up along it.

When Laura arrived in Dakota territory, the railroad had only been built to the Big Sioux River. Pa pulled the wagon farther westward, to the next place where the workers would make camp. It was thirty-five miles from anywhere.

Wild ducks and geese flew overhead in formation, honking as if to welcome the Ingallses into camp. For Mary's sake, Laura tried to describe the landscape. Most of the prairie grass grew only inches tall. But in one giant area called the Big Slough, the grasses grew six and eight feet high.

Sometimes the prairie rolled, but so gently that it was impossible to see the dips and valleys from a distance. It *looked* flat, but it wasn't.

The camp consisted of thin little houses called shanties. Built in a day or two, they were barely big enough for a family to squeeze into. And they were barely sturdy enough to keep out the powerful prairie winds.

But Laura and Ma and Pa didn't mind. This was only a temporary home. Eventually Pa would find the piece of land he wanted and stake his claim. Then, when they could afford the lumber, Pa would at last build a real house.

For several months the shanty was home while Pa worked as paymaster for the railroad crew. Then the winter winds began to blow through the Dakotas, and the workmen packed up their gear. The railroad wasn't done. But no one could build a railroad in the winter.

More important, no one could survive a Dakota winter in the railroad shanties. The walls were only thin boards covered with paper, much too flimsy to keep out the freezing winds and snow.

And once the railroad crew was gone, there would be no food, no fuel, no supplies of any kind. So how could Laura and her family survive the winter at Silver Lake? It looked as if they had no choice but to go back east.

Then, almost as if by magic, Pa made a wonderful deal with the railroad company.

Hard Winter

There was only one well-built house in the area. It was the surveyor's home, overlooking Silver Lake. Now that winter was coming, the surveyor himself was gone.

So Pa asked the railroad company to let his family spend the winter there. In exchange, he would keep an eye on the company's property during the bleak months ahead. And to everyone's joy and amazement, the railroad company agreed.

On moving day, Laura ran ahead of the wagon to the wonderful house. It stood all alone on the north shore of Silver Lake. She squealed with excitement as she opened the front door. One, two, three — there were three rooms! And each had its own window. There was an enormous stove with six burners and two ovens.

But best of all, there was a pantry, completely stocked with every kind of food they could need. Crackers, fish, salt pork, dried apples, corn meal, flour, potatoes, and beans! It was more food than

Laura had ever seen in her life. It was certainly more than enough to last the winter.

Now that all the workers had gone, Laura, Ma, Pa, Mary, Carrie, and Grace were the only people left for miles around. And now that they were alone, Laura didn't feel so little or lost anymore.

It was funny how being alone on the prairie made Laura feel safe. Most people got frightened when they were stranded in the middle of nowhere. But not Laura. As long as Ma and Pa were there, she felt secure. Home was family and family was home and that was all that mattered. Still, it was a little strange to be the only people in a desolate, silent country.

When the snows came that first winter at Silver Lake, Laura looked out upon all the glittering white stillness and felt at peace with the world.

In the daytime, she and Carrie went out together and slid across the smooth, frozen surface of the lake. Meanwhile, Mary stayed inside and told stories by the warm fire. Pa made a checkerboard so that they could play games. Ma cooked delicious meals using food from the overflowing pantry.

At night, Pa played the fiddle and they sang happy, carefree songs. It was an unforgettable time. Even when the huge buffalo wolves howled in the night, Laura didn't worry. She knew that no harm could come to them while Pa was around.

*   *   *

Laura had heard that the winters were hard in the Dakotas. But that first winter at Silver Lake was a mild one. Only once, at Christmas, did the blizzards blow so hard and cold that Laura wanted to stay inside.

But the following year was a different story.

By then, the Ingallses were living in a little shanty on the land they had claimed as their homestead. Pa had built the shanty with thick, sturdy boards, hoping it would withstand the winter. They had to live there at least six months every year, and farm the land. That was the contract Pa had signed with the government. If they did that for five years, the property would be theirs. It was 160 acres in all.

The railroad was finished now, and the town was beginning to grow. The town even had a name — De Smet. A school was built, and there were stores all along the main street, including one Pa built. He didn't want to be a storekeeper. He intended to sell it to one of the pioneer families that were arriving in town every day.

One day, however, in early October, the prairie winds began to blow. At first only a light frost covered the ground. But in the dark of night a terrible, howling storm whipped over the land and covered everything with snow.

In their shanty, Laura woke up shivering.

Snow had blown under the door and into the house. All around she could hear the low, moaning sound of the wind. It was a blizzard.

Laura couldn't speak. She was too cold. With teeth chattering, she dressed as quickly as she could. Then she wrapped Grace in some quilts and carried her to the stove. A glance at the woodpile told Laura that the temperature outside must be very, very low. They had already burned more wood that morning than they usually did in a day.

Ma couldn't believe such a blizzard had come in October. To Pa it was a warning, and its message was clear — they were facing a long hard winter.

Pa saw other warning signs, too. The muskrats built exceptionally thick houses. Geese, ducks, and swans had gone south very early in the fall. And during that early October blizzard a horrible, eerie thing had happened. Out on the prairie, some grazing cows had gotten so cold that their muzzles had frozen to the ground.

Then there was a final warning. While Pa was shopping in town, an old Indian came into the store. Wrapped in a blanket and speaking little English, the Indian warned the settlers that a hard winter was coming. He said it would be the worst one in twenty-one years.

Pa and many other settlers made a quick decision. They would spend the winter in town rather

44

than out on the prairie. The claim shanties were too thin and poorly built. Besides, if they got snowed in, they would be trapped. They would be too far from the stores in town, the only supply of food.

Luckily, Pa hadn't yet sold his store. So they all packed up their few possessions and moved to town.

Very soon, Laura found that the old Indian had been right. Never had there been a winter like the one that struck the Dakotas in 1880. One blizzard came after another, with only a few days in between. When the wind was howling, it was so loud that Laura couldn't hear herself think.

For a while, Laura and Carrie went to school in town in spite of the storms. Laura enjoyed learning and was always at the top of her class. But in November a blizzard came up so suddenly that all the children were trapped in the school building. There was no food, and barely enough coal to last the rest of the day.

Finally a man came to lead the students out — out into the freezing, whirling snow. But the storm was so violent, the snow so blinding, that even he lost his way.

Everything was a white blur. No one knew which way led to the open prairie, and which way led to town.

Snow swirled and whirled around Laura as she trudged through the storm. It was impossible to see anything in the blizzard. Laura couldn't see Carrie at all. But she clutched her sister's hand with all her might. The wind lifted them up and knocked them down.

For many long minutes it looked as though they would be lost on the prairie forever. Who knew whether they were really heading in the right direction? It seemed that they would certainly die.

In truth, Laura and the other children *were* almost lost. The man who had come to lead them home from school was heading too far north. But at the last possible minute, Laura bumped into a building. There! She had found the edge of the town.

After that, school was closed for the rest of the winter. But Laura's problems had just begun. The store in town was quickly running out of food. And so were Ma and Pa. Each day, they waited and hoped that a train would get through with a shipment of supplies. But the blizzards came so often that the tracks could never be cleared.

In January, word came that the trains had stopped running altogether. Nothing would get through until the snow melted in the spring.

Little by little, Ma's supply of food dwindled down to nothing. Laura was so hungry she felt

numb. Her thoughts were muddy; her brain seemed almost dead. Carrie, who had always been a frail child, grew even thinner. Her face was drawn and sickly white. Pa was so hungry it showed in his eyes.

Laura couldn't stand to see Pa look that way and gave him some of her food. She was fourteen years old now, old enough to know how to share and how to sacrifice.

Most families in De Smet were hungry that winter. The wealthy people had bought up the last food supplies for huge sums of money. Now there was nothing left to buy. And it would be months before the trains could get through. Many people were close to starvation.

But one person thought he could help. His name was Almanzo Wilder.

Almanzo

Almanzo Wilder and his brother Royal came from a large family in New York State. They had grown up as farm boys, but now they were grown men trying to make their way as pioneers in the west. Almanzo was twenty-four years old, and Royal was thirty-four.

Royal owned a store in town. He sold wheat, oats, and hay to feed livestock. During the long hard winter, he and Almanzo lived in the store.

But Almanzo did not plan to stay in town when the winter was over. In spring, he would move out to his homestead claim. All his life he had dreamed of being a farmer. Now there was only one thing he needed to make his dream come true. His seed wheat.

To grow a crop of wheat, every farmer needed seed. It must be planted at exactly the right time in the spring. If the trains did not come through in time, then many farmers would be unable to get seed wheat. They could not plant a crop at all that year.

But Almanzo wasn't worrying about the trains because he already had some seed wheat! He had brought many bushels of exceptional wheat with him when he moved west.

There was only one problem. All of Almanzo's dreams for the future were tied up in that wheat. He wouldn't sell it to anyone — no matter what. He hid it behind a secret wall in Royal's store. No one knew it was there.

But people were starving in De Smet during that long, hard winter. All the other wheat in town was gone. If Almanzo didn't sell his wheat, people would die of starvation.

Almanzo was a good and kind person. He couldn't let that happen. But he still didn't want to sell his seed wheat.

There was only one other choice. A rumor had been circulating that a farmer somewhere south of town had some wheat. No one knew if it was true or not, and no one knew exactly where the farmer was. Almanzo decided that he would go out in the blizzards. He would drive his horses around on the frozen prairie and try to find that wheat.

It was a crazy plan, and Almanzo knew it. When the blizzards came, they were so blinding and so fierce that people were unable even to walk across the street. But Almanzo was young and brave and willing to take the chance. And a storekeeper in town had given him money to pay for the wheat, if he could find it.

Almanzo went with a young friend, a boy named Cap Garland, from Laura's class at school. Cap was only fifteen. The journey was so dangerous that they almost froze to death. But by luck they stumbled onto a tiny shack and found the farmer they were looking for. However, the farmer did not want to sell. The wheat he had was *his* seed for spring.

But Almanzo had already shown that he would not give up easily. He talked and talked. And he offered such a high price that the farmer finally sold them his wheat. Thanks to Almanzo Wilder, many families in De Smet had food for the next three months of that long, hard winter.

Laura had seen Almanzo around town before. He caught her eye because he owned two magnificent Morgan horses. They were a matched pair — both the same deep brown color. When they galloped across the prairie pulling Almanzo's buggy, they seemed to fly like the wind.

Laura loved the energetic free spirit of Almanzo's horses. It matched her own spirit, which had always been wild and free. As for Almanzo himself,

Laura didn't think about him much. All she knew was that he had gone for the seed wheat. And he was a friend of Pa's. That was all she knew, and all she cared to know.

To Laura, Almanzo seemed like a grown man. He was twenty-four, ten years older than she was. And besides, Laura wasn't ready to think about boys. She was still something of a tomboy herself.

But Almanzo was thinking about her, and as time went by, he found a way to let her know that. A year after the hard winter, as she was leaving an evening prayer meeting at church, Almanzo asked to walk her home. She was so surprised that she didn't know what to say.

Saying practically nothing, Laura let him walk along beside her. But she felt awkward and uncomfortable, even though Ma and Pa were just ahead. The next night, the same thing happened. And then the next. Every night that week, Almanzo walked Laura home from church.

Still, Laura couldn't imagine why he was showing her so much attention. "I'm just a girl," Laura thought to herself. "And he's a grown man."

Almanzo *was* much older than Laura, and that made him patient. He was willing to wait for her to grow up. In the meantime, he tried to find ways of making himself a part of her life. A few weeks later, an opportunity came.

Like it or not — and she didn't — Laura was hired to teach school. She was only fifteen years old, and she hadn't graduated from school herself. However, young teachers were common on the frontier. She found herself teaching a class of five students. The school was in a shanty twelve miles from town.

One of the reasons Laura didn't want to teach was that it meant living away from home. She remembered how homesick she had been when she had left home to take care of Sadie Hurley.

But Laura felt she had to accept the job because it paid so well. She would earn $20 a month for two months. Then Laura would give Mary the money so she could go to a college for the blind.

So Laura went off to teach school. She lived with the Bouchie family in a small shanty on their claim. Mr. Bouchie had hired her, but Mrs. Bouchie was not happy about it. She did not want Laura there.

From the minute she arrived, Mrs. Bouchie treated her terribly. Often she wouldn't speak to Laura at all. And she screamed at her husband all the time. When Laura went to her tiny corner of the room behind a curtain, Mr. and Mrs. Bouchie

had raging arguments. Laura did not feel safe. Anger and tension hung in the air.

Laura could hardly wait to get out of the Bouchie's shanty each morning. She would walk across the snowdrifted prairie to another shanty where school was held.

There, the tension was almost as bad. Some of the students were the same age as Laura. Some were taller than she was. How could she control them if they didn't want to behave?

By the end of the week, Laura wanted to go home more than anything in the world. And somehow Almanzo Wilder knew that.

On Friday, just as it was time for Laura to dismiss school she heard sleigh bells outside. Eagerly she went to the window — and there he was! Almanzo had come, with his two beautiful brown Morgan horses!

Bundled up in a buffalo coat, Almanzo Wilder was waiting to take her home.

Sleigh Bells, Wedding Bells

Laura climbed up into Almanzo's sleigh, and he gently tucked the fur lap robes around her. Then he gave a quick signal to the Morgan horses and they were off. The sleigh bells jingled merrily as Prince and Lady trotted toward De Smet.

A look of sheer joy spread across Laura's face. Home! She was going home! She would not have to spend the long weekend with that horrible Bouchie family. Almanzo was giving her what she wanted most in the world — a safe return to the warmth and security of her family.

That weekend, Laura realized again how much she loved her parents. How lucky she was! Ma and Pa did not scream at each other the way the Bouchies did. They were always kind and considerate to one another. So were her sisters. Laura was realizing that her family was a precious gift.

For the next several weeks, Almanzo brought Laura home in his sleigh each Friday afternoon.

Each Sunday, he drove her back to the Bouchie place. Laura was grateful, knowing that if it weren't for her weekend visit, she could hardly have stood the strain of her life with the Bouchie family.

Only one thing bothered her. She did not want Almanzo to think of himself as her beau. Even though she was a teacher now, she was still only fifteen. She was a little too shy, a little too young, and a little too much of a tomboy to think about having a boyfriend.

So she told Almanzo that after her teaching job was over, she would never ride in his sleigh again. "Now that you know," she said, "you can save yourself the trouble of making these long cold drives if you want to."

The next Friday, the wind blew so furiously and the snow flew so blindingly that Laura was sure Almanzo would never come. And why should he? She had spoken so cruelly to him the week before.

But Almanzo did come. Laura nearly froze during that twelve-mile ride, but she was very grateful to him. His kindness made such an impression on her that she wrote about it later in her books.

Little by little, Laura changed her mind about Almanzo Wilder. Little by little she began to enjoy his attentions. In winter, he took her riding up and down the main street of town in his sleigh. In summer, they raced across the prairie in his buggy, trying to break in a new pair of colts.

Almanzo found a way to give Laura everything she loved most: freedom, excitement, independence, and new experiences. Knowing that she loved music, he signed them both up for singing lessons. Knowing that she loved a challenge, he let her hold the reins and drive his wild horses across the prairie.

And little by little, Laura got very used to having Almanzo around. She was seventeen now, old enough to realize that it was time to leave home. She had begun to think of Almanzo as a special person in her life. She had a special name for him, too — Manly.

So when Almanzo proposed to her after two years of courtship, Laura said yes.

There was only one condition — she would not agree to obey him. In most wedding ceremonies, brides were asked, "Do you take this man to be your husband, for better or worse, for richer or poorer, in sickness and in health, to love, honor, and obey him, as long as you both shall live?" But Laura wanted the minister to leave out the word "obey."

"I'd never expect you to obey me," Almanzo said with a tender smile.

And so the wedding took place a year later. It

was a simple ceremony, for Pa couldn't afford a big church wedding, and Almanzo couldn't either.

On the morning of August 25, 1885, Laura put on the best dress she owned. It happened to be black cashmere — not a lucky color for a wedding. But Laura didn't mind. She and Almanzo were eager to get married. And now that they had decided, there wasn't time to make a new dress.

At 10:30, Almanzo drove up in his buggy and she stepped in. Solemnly they drove to the house of Reverend Brown. In a brief private ceremony, Laura promised to love and honor Almanzo for the rest of her life — but the word obey was never used.

Afterward, wondering what the future would bring, they drove off to begin their married life together.

Heartbreak and Hope

Almanzo had built a little house for Laura on a plot of land called a tree claim. It was nothing like the Big Woods of Wisconsin. It was just ten acres planted with seedlings. Almanzo had an additional 160 acres he claimed for farming. All this land was free under the U.S. Government's Homestead Act.

But Laura hoped that if she and Almanzo watered the trees and tended them, they would one day provide cool shade from the summer sun and shelter from the powerful prairie winds.

Right now, though, the trees were only starting to grow — just like Laura's marriage.

The first year of married life was happy. But it was also hard. Laura was used to doing housework and chores, of course. But she was surprised to find out how hard it was to do *all* the work by herself, without her mother and sisters to help.

She had to cook every meal. Besides Almanzo, she often had to feed a whole crew of hungry farm workers. And when Almanzo was gone, she had to handle every kind of danger herself. Once Indians came and threatened to take things from the barn. But Laura was too independent to be afraid. She simply marched into the barn and ordered them to leave.

On the happiest days, Laura and Almanzo raced across the prairie. Laura rode a gray pony that Almanzo had bought her as a gift. She named it Trixy. Almanzo rode his own pony, named Fly. They laughed and joked together, and Laura soon proved that her pony was faster by winning every race.

Wild roses grew on the prairie. On the happiest days, Laura smelled the roses and loved them. And she rode like the wind — wild and free.

But on other days, Laura felt sick. She couldn't eat, she felt weak, and one day she fainted. Finally the doctor came out from town. He said there was nothing to worry about. She was simply going to have a baby! It was great, happy news, and Laura was glad.

The hardest thing for her, though, was accepting the fact that she was no longer a pioneer girl. Now she was a farmer's wife. Instead of going west with Pa, now she was staying put with Almanzo. It was not what Laura had dreamed of.

She did not want to spend her life doing the

never-ending farm chores. To Laura, life on a farm meant being tied down. There was something in Laura's spirit that wanted to move on, as Pa had always done — looking for a better opportunity.

And she had not promised to obey.

So she and Almanzo made a bargain. They would try farming for three years. If Almanzo did not succeed in that time, he promised to do something else — whatever Laura wanted.

As a little girl on the prairie, Laura had learned two things. First she found out that life often brought hardships. She had watched her father's wheat crops destroyed. She had heard about people who were killed by blizzards, or outlaws who wanted to steal land, or Indians. She had mourned the loss of a baby brother and seen her own dear sister go blind.

But Laura had also learned to be brave. She had seen how Pa dealt with wolves and angry railroad workers. Always, no matter what happened, Pa faced the danger calmly and with a courageous heart. Now Laura found that as a grown-up married woman, she would need all the strength and courage she had learned as a little girl. Married life was very hard.

After a year of toil, Almanzo had grown a wheat crop that looked wonderful. Then one afternoon the sky grew dark. Suddenly huge hailstones pounded down — some of them as big as eggs. They smashed Almanzo's wheat into the ground. Lying flat on the field, the wheat could not be harvested. In just twenty minutes an entire year's work had been destroyed.

And there were bills to be paid. Without telling Laura, Almanzo had gone deep into debt. They owed hundreds of dollars for farm equipment, and hundreds more on the house. Almanzo had even taken out a mortgage on the horses. There was almost nothing they owned free and clear.

The only bright moment came one cold December day. When Laura was nineteen years old, her beautiful blond baby girl was born. Shivering under many quilts, Laura looked at her tiny baby and thought back to the warm summer and the wild roses she loved so much on the prairie.

"We'll name her Rose," Laura said, and Almanzo agreed happily.

And for a while, when Rose was still a baby, the world seemed carefree and easy again. That summer Laura, Almanzo, and the baby spent most of their time outside. Laura set little Rose in a clothes basket and let her watch while she and Almanzo planted a garden. Then, when the work was done, she took Rose for rides in the horse and cart.

But the joys of summer vanished when their

second wheat crop was harvested. There had been almost no rain in the dry Dakota prairie that year, and the crop was very poor. What little profit there was from it went to pay for next year's seed, and interest on the mortgage, and doctor bills, and winter fuel. Many of the largest bills were still unpaid.

Be brave, Laura told herself. No matter what happens, look on the bright side and be brave. But the bright side always seemed to be somewhere else. All Laura could see was the darkness.

First she and Almanzo got terribly sick with diphtheria. Then, because Almanzo did not rest long enough after the illness, he suffered a stroke. His legs and hands became partly paralyzed. He could not walk properly, and couldn't use his fingers to do ordinary work.

For many months, Almanzo would fall down if he stubbed his toe. He couldn't lift his legs to walk up stairs, or even to step over a rock. Laura had to hitch up the horses for him, because his hands were too numb and stiff.

For the next two years, Laura and Almanzo were stuck between heartbreak and hope. They hoped with all their might that the next wheat crop would be a good one. But one day a hot, dry Dakota wind started to blow. By the time it stopped, the wheat crop was ruined. The hot winds had completely dried out the tiny grains of wheat.

Then Laura agreed to let Almanzo try farming for one more year. More than anything in the world she hoped that he would finally succeed. But the next summer a prairie fire came through. It burned all the wheat in the field before it had even grown.

The greatest heartbreak of all, though, came in August of 1889, when Laura was twenty-two. That year she gave birth to a second child, a boy. The baby had dark hair and looked just like Almanzo. But before she could even name him, the baby died. Heartsick, she and Almanzo put the tiny infant in their cart and drove to the cemetery south of town.

A few weeks later, still numb with grief, Laura was cooking in the little kitchen that Almanzo had built. She lit a fire in the stove and then went into the next room, closing the door behind her. Suddenly she heard an unmistakable sound — the crackling, roaring sound of fire.

She raced to the kitchen door. But she was too late. The whole kitchen was ablaze!

Quickly Laura threw a bucket of water on the fire. Then she grabbed Rose and one or two other precious things and fled to safety. Almanzo saw the fire from the fields, but he could not get back in time.

Prairie winds whipped about the house,

spreading the flames in every direction. In a matter of minutes, the entire blazing roof fell in. Their house burned to the ground.

Laura sat in the driveway sobbing and sobbing, until she thought her heart would break.

A New Start

After the fire, Laura and Almanzo were so sad that life hardly seemed worth living. Their days blurred together like one great lump of pain. Finally they decided that the only way to forget the heartache was to leave De Smet. Laura, Almanzo, and Rose went east. They needed to find rest and comfort. They needed time to recover from the grief of the fire and the death of their baby boy.

For a year they stayed with Almanzo's parents in Minnesota. Then they tried living in Florida for two years. Almanzo loved the climate because it was kind to his stiff legs. But Laura couldn't stand the heat. And she was homesick for Ma and Pa.

So they made another bargain. They would go home to Dakota, but just for a few years. They would both work and save until they had enough money to make a new start. Then they would do what Ma and Pa had always done — set out in a covered wagon to find a place they could call home.

For Almanzo, the perfect home was somewhere warmer than the Dakota prairie. Ever since his stroke, he had hated the cold. He also wanted a place where he could raise horses and chickens and have a farm.

For Laura, the ideal place was somewhere with trees. She wanted to live where the landscape was beautiful. And she already had an idea where that might be. She had heard of a place called The Land of the Big Red Apple. It was a nickname for Mansfield, Missouri. Laura had seen pictures of the town, and of huge red apples growing there. That must be a wonderful land of plenty!

So in July of 1894, after working and saving money for two years, Laura and Almanzo set out from De Smet on their journey to find a new home. Carefully, they packed their few precious belongings into Almanzo's two-seated hack. The hack was a wagon with a black canvas top and side curtains.

Laura and Almanzo rode on the seat, high up in front. Rose, who was seven years old, rode in back. Now Rose was the little girl going off to explore the vast countryside with her parents — just as Laura had done so many times when she was young.

On covered wagon trips, the most precious possessions were wrapped in blankets and tucked carefully in among the other things. That way they wouldn't be harmed by the bumping and jostling as the wagon rolled over rough roads, or no roads at all.

When Laura was little, Pa's most precious possession had been his fiddle. Now Laura's treasure was a polished wooden writing desk that Almanzo had made for her. She took special care to wrap it. Then she set it gently in among the clothes, food, and pots that were already packed and ready to go.

The desk was beautifully made. It was a box that opened on small hinges to reveal several small compartments and a slanted surface for writing. In one compartment, Laura kept paper and letters she had received. In another, there was room for a bottle of ink and her special pearl-handled pen.

But on this trip there was one more item carefully tucked inside the desk. It was a one hundred dollar bill.

In those days, a hundred dollars was worth much more than it is now — it was the money Laura and Almanzo had saved from all their months of work. It was the money that would give them a new start in the Land of the Big Red Apple. Nothing must happen to that precious hundred dollar bill.

Rose knew the bill was there, but she had been warned not to tell anyone. Not even Paul or George, the two young Cooley boys who were going along on the trip. Mr. and Mrs. Cooley were friends of Laura's and Almanzo's, and they were going to Missouri, too. They were driving their own wagons on the journey south.

In her heart, Laura hoped desperately that Mansfield would be the perfect home she and Almanzo were looking for. But in her head, she knew that it might not be. They might keep on searching, as Pa had — always trying to find a better spot over the next hill. Or beyond the far horizon.

As they set out on the journey, Laura began to keep a diary. It was the first time she had ever done that. In fact, it was the first time she had ever written *anything* more than a letter or a school essay. It was almost like the days of long ago, when she had described the landscape for Mary. Once again, she was painting pictures with words.

Each day she wrote down how the crops were doing. She made notes about the price of land. And she kept track of the temperature inside the wagon, which was often above 100 degrees. Laura and Almanzo probably didn't know that the black canvas cover on their wagon was making it much hotter inside.

Day after day, Laura looked at the hot, dry prairie. There wasn't a tree in sight. Not one. But finally one Saturday Almanzo pulled the wagon into a campsite along the James River. There were trees growing near the water, and the crops looked better, too.

Soon the Wilders and the Cooleys started on their journey again. Sometimes they stopped so that Almanzo and Mr. Cooley could earn money doing field work. But usually they pressed on, eager to reach the Land of the Big Red Apple.

As they went farther and farther, Laura was beginning to wonder if they were headed in the right direction. Nearly every day they passed other covered wagons traveling the other way. They were coming from Missouri and heading north, toward the Dakotas. What did it mean?

Finally, after forty-five days, they reached the Ozarks. The landscape was rocky but very beautiful — just what Laura had dreamed of. There were trees everywhere, and rolling grassy hills often planted with strawberries. The air was much cooler than it had been on the prairie. Almanzo thought Missouri was lovely, too.

Laura immediately knew that this was the paradise she had wanted. Now all they had to do was find the right farm.

They camped in a forest outside Mansfield. Every day Almanzo went to look for a homesite. Finally he came back with great news. He had found the perfect spot! Of course Laura must see the farm before they bought it. She left Rose with Mrs. Cooley and went with Almanzo to look at it.

The farm was forty acres of land rolling up

and down over a rocky ridge. Then it sloped off to a spring of clear, pure water. Best of all, there were trees — trees as far as Laura could see! And there were four hundred little apple trees waiting to be planted. There was even a log cabin in a clearing at the very top of the hill.

It was just a little house — but Laura was used to little houses. This would be a perfect place to begin their lives again.

Glowing with excitement, Laura hurried to get into her finest dress. She and Almanzo were going to the bank that very day, to buy the farm. Carefully she took the writing desk from its safe place in the wagon. But when she opened it, the hundred dollar bill was gone!

Be brave, Laura told herself. There must be an explanation. The money couldn't possibly be lost!

But it was. No matter how hard they looked, Laura and Almanzo could not find it. It was not in any of the compartments. It was not among the papers or envelopes. They took everything out of the desk and shook it. Still the precious bill did not turn up.

There was an awful, sickening silence as the hours wore on. All their hopes and dreams had suddenly disappeared. And then Laura began to wonder if Rose was to blame. Had Rose played with the bill? Laura asked her daughter again and again.

Had she told anyone about it? For an instant, Laura wondered aloud whether the Cooleys might have taken it. But no. They were friends. They could not have done such a terrible thing.

Days went by. It seemed like an eternity. Laura was heartsick and silent. Almanzo looked for work. The food began to run out. Rose feared that she and her parents would starve.

And then one day, just as abruptly as it had disappeared, the hundred dollar bill returned. Rose never did find out exactly what happened. All her mother ever told her was that it had been in the writing desk the whole time.

Once the hundred dollar bill was found, Laura and Almanzo were able to buy the farm in Mansfield. And it turned out to be a jewel — a diamond in the rough. Laura saw that it would take work, but eventually she would have a better little house than any she had lived in before. From her windows she would look out on beautiful views of sun and mountains and sky. The apple trees would bloom in the spring. The orchards would be laden with fruit in the fall.

And everything they needed to build a little house was right there on the land.

Famous Daughter Rose

For the next fifteen years, Laura and Almanzo worked very hard. Clearing the rocky hills was difficult. They had to dig huge boulders out of the ground before they could even begin to plant the apple trees. They had to cut all their own lumber from trees growing on their own land. They had to raise all their own food by planting crops and tending chickens. It took many years to build the house of their dreams. They started with just one room, then added another room every year or so until there were ten rooms in all.

But despite the hard work, Laura and Almanzo were happy in Mansfield. They would stay on Rocky Ridge Farm for the rest of their lives.

Meanwhile, amidst berry bushes and fruit trees, little Rose was growing up. Soon it would be her turn to be a pioneer — and to have her own adventures. But first she must go to school.

Rose was a bright child who loved everything

about words. She taught herself to read at the age of three. At eight, she rode to school on a donkey named Spookendyke. As she rode, she made up her own language — called Fispooko.

But at school, Rose was bored. The classes taught in Mansfield weren't challenging enough for her. She often stayed home because she was "mad at the teacher." She complained that he made them do stupid things, and didn't understand half of what he was teaching. And Laura, who had never liked following unfair rules, let her daughter defy the school.

When Rose stayed home, she studied on her own. She borrowed books from wealthy families in town. She studied algebra and history. She read poems, novels, and plays. She was educating herself, and she liked it that way.

Rose began to dream that she would be a writer when she grew up.

But first she wanted to graduate from high school. Laura knew that Rose wasn't learning enough at the school in Mansfield. Then one day one of Almanzo's sisters arrived for a visit and suggested that Rose come live with her. Laura quickly said yes.

The sister lived in Crowley, Louisiana, and Rose was happy to go there. She felt cramped and confined by the small-town life of Mansfield. She didn't like the drudgery of chores on the farm. And besides, she loved the challenge of going to school in Crowley. To graduate, she had to learn three years of Latin in one year — which was no problem for her. She even composed a poem in Latin that she read at graduation.

And then Rose set off to see the world.

Laura and Almanzo worried about her, of course. In 1904 it was not common for an eighteen-year-old girl to travel alone, or even live alone. It shocked most people. Laura knew there would be talk. People would say that nice girls didn't do such things. Nice girls didn't have careers. Nice girls got married and let their husbands take care of them.

But Laura understood that Rose had the same rebellious spirit she had. Laura understood the desire to seek adventure, wild and free. So she let her daughter do what she wanted to do.

Rose's first job was as a telegraph operator for Western Union. At first she worked in Kansas City, sending and receiving telegraph messages. Then she moved around the country, working in various Western Union offices until finally the company sent her to San Francisco.

What a great city that was! The year was 1908, and Rose was very happy. She was earning good money, and she was independent and free. There was only one problem — she was getting bored with telegraphy.

So she talked her way into a job selling real estate. She was the first woman to do that anywhere in California. She made large commissions, and was a success. And she fell in love with a real estate salesman named Gillette Lane.

Soon Rose married Gillette, and she became Rose Wilder Lane. They enjoyed life because they were both earning a great deal of money. They both liked to spend money, too. But the real estate business dried up, and Rose had to find something else to do.

She had always wanted to be a writer. Could she make a success of it now? Luckily, she knew someone at a newspaper. Her friend wrote the woman's page for the San Francisco *Bulletin*. So Rose managed to sell a few stories to the paper. And even though they were simple love stories, her natural talent with words made her an immediate success. Soon she was offered a full-time job, doing serious reporting. Rose Wilder Lane had become a newspaperwoman.

Meanwhile, in Mansfield, Laura was getting a reputation as an expert at managing chickens. She was so good, in fact, that farmers all over Missouri were asking her to come and speak about raising poultry.

But one day she was too busy to go to the farmers' meeting. So she wrote down her poultry speech and sent it in to be read by someone else. One person in the audience was an editor on the *Missouri Ruralist,* a publication for farmers. He thought Laura had writing talent and offered her a job.

Soon she was writing regularly about her hens, about farm life in the Ozarks, and about building her dream house on Rocky Ridge Farm.

By 1915, both Laura and her daughter were writers. Rose was well on her way to becoming famous around the world, and Laura was famous among the farmers of Missouri. Her years of writing the Little House books were still far ahead in the future.

Then one day Laura got a letter from her daughter. Rose was now one of the leading feature writers for the San Francisco *Bulletin.* This meant that she spent her days wandering through the city, looking for interesting topics to write about. She ate lunch in nice cafes. She earned good money as a writer, and she and Gillette lived very well.

Rose loved her mother so much that she wanted to share this exciting life with her. She also wanted to help Laura with her own writing career. So she wrote to Laura, begging her to come visit San Francisco in 1915. She wanted Laura to see the World's Fair. Laura agreed.

The World's Fair was a sensational exhibition — like nothing Laura had ever seen before. Magnificent buildings stood all along the waterfront. One was decorated with thousands of rhinestone "jewels." There were carnival rides and live kangaroos, grand fountains and splendid gardens. Astonishing exhibits from nearly every country in the world were on display.

Laura came by train, and Rose paid all the expenses. It was a visit Laura would never forget. She ate foods like salmon, French tarts, and a kind of English biscuit with raisins in it, called a scone. At the age of forty-eight, she put her feet into the ocean for the first time, and felt dazzled by it. She saw fireworks every single night — spectacular displays that took her breath away.

It was all so wonderful, so dramatic and exciting, that Laura stayed and stayed. She stayed far longer than she had originally planned — two and a half months in all.

But Laura also watched how hard Rose worked. She saw that when Rose was working on an article for a deadline, she ignored her mother completely, and spent every minute writing.

In a letter Laura wrote to Almanzo, she said: "The more I see of how Rose works, the better satisfied I am to raise chickens. I intend to try to do some writing that will count, but I would not be driven by the work as she is for anything and I do not see how she can stand it."

The "Little House" Books

Laura was thrilled by her San Francisco trip. But she was also happy to come home to Almanzo and Rocky Ridge Farm. She could not imagine herself chasing around the world after newspaper stories the way Rose did. To Laura, the most precious thing in life had always been home.

So for the next several years she was satisfied just to write short articles about farm life — and letters home to her Ma and sisters Mary, Carrie, and Grace. When Pa was dying in 1902, Laura made the journey all the way to De Smet to be at his side when he died. And on a few other occasions, Laura had visited her sisters and Ma. She made the long train trips to De Smet on her own. But those visits were rare. Mostly Laura relied on her letters to let the family know that she still loved them and missed them so much.

By now, Carrie was a career woman, working as a typesetter for a newspaper in Keystone, South Dakota. She was married to a widower who had two children of his own. Mary, who wasn't married, lived at home with Ma where she wrote poetry and lived a quiet life. And Grace was married to a farmer who lived in a small town near De Smet. They took care of Mary and Ma whenever either of the women became ill.

Meanwhile, Rose was becoming increasingly well-known as a writer. She rode an airplane while strapped to the wing, and then described the experience. She interviewed Henry Ford, the great automobile tycoon, and wrote the first biography of his life.

A few years later, Rose and her husband decided to get divorced. After that she began to travel the world. She lived in New York City and wrote for magazines. She went to Europe after World War I, and sent back stories from France, Italy, Yugoslavia, Egypt, Albania, and many other places.

Finally she went home to Rocky Ridge Farm and lived with Laura, whom she called "Mama Bess." There she wrote novels about the people she had known in the small towns of the rural midwest.

In the 1930s Rose returned to New York City to write for magazines once again. This time she wrote fiction based on the stories Laura had told her about growing up in pioneer days. These pieces were published in the *Saturday Evening Post* and were a great success. But Rose did not want to take all the credit. She realized that Laura could be a wonderful fiction writer, too, if only she would try.

So Rose wrote to her mother, asking her to put the stories from her childhood down on paper. And that letter was a turning point in the life of Laura Ingalls Wilder.

Laura was in her sixties now, and had lived a fascinating life. But her happiest memories were of her childhood, and of the pioneer days with Pa.

Laura had loved Pa, perhaps more than anything else in the world. Now all she had to remember him by were the wonderful stories he told her when she was a child. As a tribute to her beloved father, she would pass along Pa's stories to other children. In a way, Laura felt that by writing she could make Pa live again.

She sat down by the window in her little corner study and began. Using a pencil, and writing on thick tablets of school paper, Laura covered the front and back of every sheet. She had been taught not to waste, so she wrote all the way across each page, leaving no margins. She wasted none of her memories, either. She wrote everything in just one book — her father's stories, together with her entire life as a pioneer girl.

It was Laura's first attempt at writing a book. She called it *Pioneer Girl* and sent it off to her daughter in New York. Rose helped her mother by edit-

ing the manuscript, but she was unable to find a publisher for her mother's lengthy autobiography.

With Rose's help and encouragement, Laura tried again. This time she narrowed the focus of her book. She wrote only about her earliest childhood memories — her memories of life in the Big Woods.

Of course Laura had lived in the Big Woods twice — once when she was just a baby, and then again starting at the age of four. But now she changed the facts a little. She had learned that a good story must be simple and clear.

So she left out the fact that young Laura had already moved several times. That part didn't really matter. What mattered was that the events and the feelings were all true. She had written from the heart.

When Rose showed this book to an editor at a publishing company called Alfred A. Knopf, the response was quite different. The editor thought Laura's story was special, but Laura needed to do some work on it. "These stories are good," the editor told Laura, "but put some meat on them." Laura reworked the stories, but she ended up having to find a new editor. The children's book department at Alfred A. Knopf was closed to cut costs during the Great Depression.

The new editor worked in the children's book

department at another publishing company called Harper and Brothers. She read the manuscript as she rode the train from New York City to her house in the suburbs. She got so wrapped up in the stories that she missed her stop. She simply forgot to get off the train.

The editor immediately knew the book was good. It had held her attention, and she thought it would hold the attention of young readers everywhere.

The book was called *Little House in the Big Woods,* and was finally published in the spring of 1932. Although it had taken several years to write, it was an overnight success. Laura was then sixty-five years old.

When Laura wrote her first book, she thought it would be her last. But children everywhere loved it so much that they demanded more. She was amazed at this success because, as she later said, "I never graduated from anything!"

Next, she decided to write *Farmer Boy,* the story of Almanzo's childhood. Again, her first draft was not perfect. She had to revise the book before it was published. And again, the finished book was so wonderful that readers all over America demanded more.

Now Laura knew that she really *was* a writer,

and that she would have to write more and more stories to keep her young audience satisfied. For her third book, *Little House on the Prairie,* Laura relied on the stories that Pa and Ma and Mary had told. Even though Laura really had lived in Indian Territory, she was only two and three years old at the time. She didn't remember the wolves or the Indians herself.

But she recalled enough of what the family told her to make it all come to life for her readers. And again the book was an instant success.

After that, the memories came rushing back. Laura found that the more she concentrated on the past, the more she could find there. She certainly remembered Plum Creek and the year of the grass-hoppers. She certainly remembered the long, hard winter when they almost starved to death. But as she looked back over her life, she decided that she did not want to write about the unhappy times. What was important were the times when she had felt warm and safe and loved. The times that had shaped her character and given her a true under-standing of what was valuable in life.

Laura published eight Little House books in all, one right after another. Each one took about two years to write. They covered her life from child-hood to marriage. In 1943, Laura published her last book, *These Happy Golden Years,* at the age of 76.

*   *   *

Laura's final years were spent much as she had lived her whole life. She and Almanzo were completely content, enjoying the farm they had built from nothing. She still made her own butter and worked in the garden. In the evenings, the two of them sat quietly by the fireplace, reading magazines or playing a game of cribbage. And when Laura was invited to a club meeting in town, she still baked gingerbread from her own recipe and brought it along. Her recipe is in the back of this book.

With her courage and determination to be brave and go on, no matter what, Laura outlived all her family members except Rose.

Almanzo died at the age of ninety-two. Eight years later, on February 10, 1957, Laura Ingalls Wilder died. It was just three days after her birthday. She was ninety years old.

After Laura died, three more books were published under her name. First, Rose found the diary her mother had kept during the trip from South Dakota to Mansfield, when they were looking for a new home. The diary was published just as Laura wrote it and was called *On the Way Home*.

Then, there was another discovery after Rose died—a packet of Laura's letters to Almanzo from San Francisco. Laura had asked Almanzo to save them because she thought someday she might write an article about her trip. They were published under the title *West From Home*.

And finally, another Little House manuscript was found. It described the early years of Laura's marriage and told of all her sorrows — the lost crops, the fire, and the infant boy who died. Laura never finished it and probably never intended it to be printed. It was, after all, a sad story, and she believed that the Little House series should have a happy ending.

But readers kept asking "What happened next?" So the manuscript was finally published as *The First Four Years*.

At the end of her life, Laura had become a world-famous children's book author. Libraries were named for her, and awards were given to her. And children everywhere wrote letters to her.

In her letters back, Laura said, "The real things haven't changed; they can never change. It is still best to be honest and truthful; to make the most of what we have; to be happy with simple pleasures and to be cheerful and have courage when things go wrong."

1867   Laura Elizabeth Ingalls is born on February 7 in the little house in the Big Woods.

1868   In July, Pa moves the family west. The journey takes almost two months. Laura is only one-and-a-half.

1869   Pa settles in Indian territory and builds the little house on the prairie. Later, this land would become part of Kansas.

1871   At the age of four, Laura travels by covered wagon back to the little house in the Big Woods. These were some of her earliest memories.

1874   Once again Pa moves the family westward. They stop on the banks of Plum Creek, outside Walnut Grove, Minnesota. Over the next few years, Laura will move nine times, eventually returning to Walnut Grove.

1879 Ma and Pa decide to go west for the last time. They are the very first settlers in the town of De Smet, Dakota Territory. Later, the area would be called South Dakota.

1880– 1881 Laura's family endures the famous long winter, lasting seven months. When food and fuel run out in the town, they almost starve. Almanzo Wilder saves a number of families by risking his life in the blizzards to search for wheat.

1885 Laura, age eighteen, and Almanzo, age twenty-eight, are married quietly on August 25.

1886 Rose Wilder is born.

1889 Laura has another baby who dies when he is only a few days old. Two weeks later, her house burns down.

1894 Laura, Almanzo, and Rose make a journey by covered wagon, looking for a new home. They go from South Dakota to Mansfield, Missouri. The trip takes forty-five days.

1911   At the age of forty-four, Laura becomes a writer. Her first article is published in a farm journal, the *Missouri Ruralist.* She writes under the name of Mrs. Wilder.

1915   Laura's daughter Rose invites her to visit San Francisco and see the World's Fair.

1932   Laura's first book, *Little House in the Big Woods,* is published by Harper and Brothers.

1933   *Farmer Boy* is published.

1935   *Little House on the Prairie* is published.

1937   *On the Banks of Plum Creek* is published.

1939   *By the Shores of Silver Lake* is published.

1940   *The Long Winter* is published. Laura wants to call it *The Hard Winter,* but the editors object. They say children should not be told that anything was hard.

1941   *Little Town on the Prairie* is published.

1943   *These Happy Golden Years* is published. The original version of this book says it is the end of the Little House story.

1949   Almanzo dies at the age of ninety-two.

1953   Newly illustrated editions of all the Little House books are published, with pictures by Garth Williams.

1957   Laura dies on February 10 at the age of ninety, three days after her birthday.

Laura Ingalls Wilder's Gingerbread

½ cup brown sugar blended with
½ cup lard or other shortening
½ cup molasses blended with this
2 teaspoons baking soda in 1 cup boiling water

(Be sure cup is full of water after foam is run off into cake mixture.)

To 3 cups of flour have added one teaspoon each of the following spices: ginger, cinnamon, allspice, nutmeg, cloves; and ½ teaspoon salt. Sift all into cake mixture and mix well.

Add lastly 2 well-beaten eggs.

The mixture should be quite thin.

Bake in a moderate oven for thirty minutes.

Raisins and/or candied fruit may be added and a chocolate frosting adds to the goodness.